I0436961

A
HELPING
HAND

A Simple Way That Anyone

**From a Child of 5 to a
Senior of 95, a Family, a
Group or Organization or a
Business of any Size**

Can Give Less Money to Charity

**And Get Back More, Much
More Than They Give.**

A Helping Hand Foundation, Inc.
Robert O. Doucette

A HELPING HAND

A new simple way to give to others

Where - You Give Less Dollars

You See How Your Gift
is Used

You Make a Difference

You Gain Personal Joy.

A Helping Hand Foundation, Inc.
Robert O. Doucette
www.A-HelpingHand.org

AuthorHouse™
1663 Liberty Drive, Suite 200
Bloomington, IN 47403
www.authorhouse.com
Phone: 1-800-839-8640

AuthorHouse™ UK Ltd.
500 Avebury Boulevard
Central Milton Keynes, MK9 2BE
www.authorhouse.co.uk
Phone: 08001974150

First published by AuthorHouse 8/7/2006

ISBN: 1-4259-4433-7 (sc)

Printed in the United States of America
Bloomington, Indiana

This book is printed on acid-free paper.

To purchase additional copies of this book contact:
Author House
1663 Liberty Drive, Suite 200
Bloomington, Indiana 47403
888-519-5121
www.AuthorHouse.com

Bloomington, IN  Milton Keynes, UK

This book is dedicated to - - -

The following people who have brought joy into my life

and

Continue to do so - - - everyday.

My wife	Pauline (Me Mom to her grandchildren)
My children	Jim, Julie, Jane
My grandchildren	Michael, Erik, Troy, Brianna, Iain

Foreword

Have you ever asked yourself or wondered…

What's the purpose of my life? Should there be more meaning than just the accumulation of material goods and the pursuit of recreation?

Why do I often feel that I'm not giving enough money to charitable causes? Is it because I don't see the results?

Is it because I feel I can't make a real difference, so I do nothing or very little?

How can I do more to help, to make a difference in the world when I feel I don't have the time, the education, the contacts, or the money to do so?

If you have ever asked yourself any one of these questions, this book and its simple mes-

sage and a few simple steps will show you
how to:

- Give a new purpose and meaning to
  your life.

- Allow you to see exactly how your
  charitable donations are used.

- Really see if you're making a difference
  in the lives of children or people.

- And, allow you to receive back more than
  you give through your charitable giving.

The book and its simple message will show
any person from a child of 5 to a senior of 95,
a family, a group, an organization, or a business of any size how to give with a purpose,
really make a difference, and get back more
than you give.

This book explains that true charitable giving is not about money, but is about giving to
a cause you believe in, providing some seed
money, combined with your time and talent to
get specific results.

It's surprisingly simple.
It's surprisingly easy.

This is a simple idea that you can try and see for yourself the personal satisfaction and benefits you will realize.

You can really gain a lot and you can't lose anything so why not give it a try?

A HELPING HAND

The scene was Lido's Restaurant on Central Street in Plainville, NY and it was about noontime, it was time for the four friends to continue their friendships that began many years ago.

Ray arrives at the restaurant first; he is in his early 60s and is a retired purchasing agent of a large company. Shortly after Ray arrives, two of the other friends come in; Bob has been teaching the sixth grade for 15 years and Tom is a local pediatrician. Finally, about 5 minutes later, the fourth friend, Ed arrives. He is an accountant with a medium size business in the Town of Plainville, a business employing about 200 people.

After each of them sits at the table that they've occupied every Wednesday for the last twelve years, they exchange the usual pleasantries, scan the menu and place their orders for lunch.

Not only do these luncheons renew and strengthen their friendships, each week they have a custom of discussing various aspects of their lives, whether its the activities of their children, problems at work, and religious activities, family activities, recreation activities, etc. Well, you get the idea.

As soon as they settle in and order their meals from the waitress, Ed, the accountant, starts the discussion by announcing, "I'm wondering if we could talk about giving to charities - you know, charitable giving?"

Ed relates, "Recently in the news there was a very horrible disaster which killed thousands of people." Bob said, "I know, as soon as I read about it I knew I had to donate money immediately, so I got my checkbook and wrote a check for $100 and immediately sent it to the American Red Cross. I had to do something to help."

Ray quickly joined in and said "I felt the same way, that this was such a great disaster that I also felt the need to send a check to help. I sent one to Save the Children."

Tom, the pediatrician, said "I read a short time later that hundreds of millions of dollars had been contributed from around the world to this very needy cause and I started to wonder how my $200 donation was being used? Did it really make a difference? Tom also said, "I've often felt this way about charitable checks that I have written, often wondering later if my contribution really made a difference? I hope it did, but I'm not sure."

Bob asked, "If I understand you, you often feel like you're not doing enough, but at the same time feel that what you're doing really doesn't make a difference?" Ray chimed in and said, "I see so many needs in the world, so many children that need help sometimes right in our own communities, whether its abused children, homeless children, children in foster care, children without proper education I often feel that I should do more, but I'm retired and on a tight budget." Ed joined in and said, "I know how you feel because I often feel the same way, that I should do more, but feel that the needs are so great that whatever I do would not be enough."

The clear consensus among all four friends was that they all felt they should do more, but they weren't sure how to. Ray said, "I'd like to make a difference in somebody else's life but really don't know how to. If I had more money to give I think it would make all the difference." Bob mentioned, "I feel that charitable giving in is an obligation, something I really feel guilty about if I don't do anything."

Ed chimed in and said, "You know, sometime we ought to talk to my brother-in-law Larry. He helps a lot of children with his charitable giving. Why, just last Christmas he arranged for over 200 toys to be given to needy children in the area. My wife told me that he has helped a lot of foster children in various ways. He's donated a lot of books to the children's Head Start program and also given games and stuffed animals to sick children in the hospital."

Ray stated, "Well, he must have a lot of money to give away if he can do all of that." But Ed replied, "No, he doesn't. I think he gives less than I do. I know his income is substantially less than mine and he has two more children than I have." "Also," Ed said, "the few times I've talked to Larry about his charitable activities he beams and tells me how satisfying it is to him. He says that his charitable activity brings him a personal satisfaction that was missing when he donated only money." Bob said, "Larry sounds like someone we should talk to so that we can find out what's different in his approach that makes his charitable giving so satisfying and enriching to him." Ray immediately agreed.

Tom asked, "Ed, do you think Larry would come to lunch next week to speak with us?" Ed answered, "Sure, you'll like Larry, he's very outgoing, a real people person, and I'm sure he'd be glad to share his secrets of charitable giving. I bet we'll learn a lot from him."

The check comes and the four friends split it, leave a generous tip for the waitress, and leave with Ed's promise to invite Larry to meet next Wednesday at Lido's. Each of them is looking forward to talking with Larry and learning about his effective charitable giving.

That night Ed called Larry and explained the conversation that took place at Lido's – about the lack of fulfillment in their charitable giving and the invitation for next Wednesday's lunch. Larry quickly accepted saying, "You know how much my Charitable Assignment means to me, of course I'll be there." Ed hung up the phone thinking, "What did he mean by Charitable Assignment?" The week passed quickly and the four friends were sitting at their favorite table at Lido's when Larry came in. Ed stood up and introduced him to Ray, Bob, and Tom. Ray said, "Larry, thank you for joining us today, we're looking forward to hearing about your successful charitable activities." Tom quipped, "As a matter of fact, pick anything on the menu, this lunch is on us!" The four friends laughed and nodded in agreement. While reviewing the menu, Ray, Bob, and Tom learn that Larry is as automotive service technician at one of the new car dealers and has been working there for about 20 years. He is a solid citizen, very well liked, married and has four terrific children. His wife is a stay at home mother.

Bob said, "Our charitable giving has been primarily a process of writing checks and the four of us agree that we all feel inadequate, that we're not doing enough." Ed reminded them, "And, don't forget, we don't know how our money is being used and whether it made any difference and we'd like to change this." Ray added, "And because of these unknowns we don't really get any lasting personal satisfaction from giving." They invite Larry to explain his methods.

While the waitress brought their meals, Larry started to explain how he achieves personal satisfaction through charitable giving and how he accomplishes more with smaller donations by saying, "For many years, like the four of you, my charitable giving was simply a process of writing a check to one or more organizations when I felt I could afford to." He continued, "I wasn't very satisfied with what was being accomplished because I never could see the difference my donations were making, and because of this, I felt somewhat inadequate."

"How did you turn that around?" asked Tom.

Larry replied, "I started to read about charitable organizations that accomplished a great deal and was impressed when I discovered as I read their stories that there were only four basic, easy and simple steps being used by ordinary people that allowed them to accomplish much more in their charitable giving. In most cases, with less money than I was contributing."

Bob asked, "Will you tell us about these four steps?" Larry's response was, "I think I could be of most help to the four of you if I explain one step each week, have you reflect on the step and make some decisions and we'll discuss it at our next luncheon." Ed added, "Devoting a week to one step will keep it simple and easy just as you had discovered." Ray, Tom, Ed and Bob were eager to learn what the first step would be.

Larry said, "Let me tell you about one of the amazing stories I read that helped me define these four steps. Aubyn Burnside and her brother Welland, learned through their older sister that foster children who had been taken from their parents for various reasons often had to move from foster home to foster home and to make matters worse, all they had to put their belongings in were trash bags for these moves." "That's sad," Ray said.

Larry continued, "Aubyn and Welland decided they wanted to do something to help these foster children. They started by asking their mother if she had any unused suitcases, and she had a few. Encouraged, they knocked on neighborhood doors, posted notices in schools and libraries asking people to donate their extra or unused suitcases so they could be given to foster children." Larry noticed the four men were silent, so he continued, "Within a few weeks they collected almost 175 suitcases and brought them to a social service agency. The story was reported in local and eventually regional newspapers, the story spread and it wasn't long before Aubyn started getting requests from others in surrounding cities and towns, even in other states to do the same thing." Bob said, "How clever, these kids heard of a need and came up with a simple solution." Ed asked, "How did she answer the requests?" Larry answered, "Aubyn and Welland wrote a simple manual on how to collect pre-owed suitcases for foster children, and she later established a website which contained the same instructions. In less than five years there were chapters of the organization that she calls, "Suitcases for Kids" in all of our 50 states and a few foreign countries."

Bob said, "Isn't it amazing that those kids achieved so much, really made a difference." "That just it," Larry said, from reading this story and the amazing results with practically no money, I determined that the first step in effective charitable giving had to be focus."

Ray said, "That's what Aubyn and Welland did – focus on collecting used suitcases for foster kids." Larry added. "Because of their efforts thousands of foster children were helped throughout the country." Tom said, "And don't forget, in a few foreign countries too."

Larry wrapped up the first story by saying, "The most impressive part of this story was that when Aubyn started to collect suitcases for foster children she was 11 years old and her brother Welland was 7."

Ray said, "That's an impressive story. Two children made such a difference in the lives of so many other children." Ed added, "We see what you mean by the first step and the need for a determined and specific focus."

Since their lunchtime was running out they agreed that for their next meeting each of them would have decided on a focused need in their community. To help, Larry suggested, "Why not think of the needs of children - in hospitals, handicapped, homeless, their educational needs. Focus on some particular need that would have meaning to you. Don't be concerned at this point about how much you could do, but rather just as Aubyn and Welland did, decide on something specific that you could do in our community to make a difference in the lives of one or a few children."

STEP ONE

Focus

To be effective

To make a difference

You must focus – focus – focus

On one need

On one way you can help.

During that week each of the four friends found themselves thinking about the one area they'd like to focus on – it was the first step, focus. Larry had explained at the meeting that he would lead them through the four simple steps and that they would be choosing to do a "Charitable Assignment". Unlike other assignments, this would be one that would be chosen by them and they would make it fit in with their time that they had to give. Larry had said, "That this Charitable Assignment would show each of you the truth to the statement that is it better to give than to receive."

Ray and Tom were early next Wednesday and were anxious to renew their discussion of focus, and Ed and Bob arrived shortly. All of them were anxious to exchange their ideas on what they had decided to focus on and to learn the second step of the Charitable Assignments.

Larry arrived just a few minutes after noon. Once again, pleasantries were exchanged and the friends placed their orders for lunch.

Larry asked, "Who would like to explain their ideas on focus?" Ray began, "Well, I was reading an article about homelessness, then spoke with a few social workers and learned there are homeless children and families right here in Plainville." Tom stated, "There's probably nothing more devastating to a family than to find itself homeless." "You're right Tom, that's why I decided that my focus for this Charitable Assignment would be to help one homeless family," said Ray.

Bob said, "I also checked with a social worker and did a little reading at the library and discovered, much to my surprise, there are, in America today, over 12 million children who live in a state of poverty. I found this so very hard to believe considering the wealth and affluence we have in America that I decided my focus would be on helping one, two or a few children living in poverty here, in Plainville."

Tom then said, "I would like to focus on helping children improve their education in someway. I believe children could use help from all of us in enhancing their education, particularly some of the kids who may not have the advantages others do. So, my emphasis, my focus, will be on helping children in some way with their education."

Ed was thrilled and said, "Tom, I decided on contributing to children's education. Were you thinking of a specific age group? I was considering high school." Tom replied, "I was leaning toward toddlers and young people." Ed said, "I am in complete agreement about enhancing education because I believe that education is the key that unlocks the door to successful and enriching lives. That too will be my focus, enhancing the educational process." Bob interjected, "I have a couple of ideas that might help the two of you, give me a call later this week if you're interested."

It had only taken them a few minutes to explain their decision on focus and the waitress arrived with their meals. Each of them took a few minutes to eat and as coffee and dessert arrived they were ready to listen to Larry to learn the second step in the Charitable Assignment process.

Larry said, "Well, it's obvious you were sincere in changing your approach to charitable giving because you took the time over the past week to reflect on a focused mission." Larry continued, "The process of focusing on a particular need is extremely important - it helps us to become much more aware of the needs in our community. In today's world with its constant busyness, well, there's a danger that each of us is losing touch with, and losing awareness of, the needs in our country, in our own states, in our cities, towns, and in fact, in our own backyards. Choosing a focus forces us to become more aware."

Larry said in explaining the second step, "Once again, I would like to tell you a real life story of a hero in the charitable world. A person who much like Aubyn and her brother Welland started a process which ended up helping many people. She was truly the spark that that started a bonfire."

"A few years ago," Larry said, "I read about a housewife in Colorado, a Karen Louks, who while reading the newspaper one day read about Laura, a young girl in a Colorado children's hospital who was undergoing cancer treatment and her touching story about how much her security blanket was of help to her as she was undergoing the chemotherapy."

"Karen had always loved to knit and after reading that touching story, which brought her to tears, she wondered how many other children could be helped in their recovery from an illness by having a security blanket to hold. She started knitting a few security blankets and brought them to the children's hospital. Karen was truly moved by the effect it had on the children in the hospital. The local newspaper reported the story of what Karen had done to help these children and she started getting calls from other women, all of whom were knitters as she was, asking how they could help. Later she decided to establish a website with instructions on knitting and the account of her story and how she was motivated by the story of Laura."

Larry continued, "Karen saw her idea grow as she had more and more contacts with women who loved to knit and who loved what she had done and wanted to do the same. Later she decided to establish her own nonprofit organization to do what she could to spread the idea and today, just a few short years after the story of Laura appeared in the Colorado newspaper, there are chapters all over the United States in many cities and towns with hundreds of volunteers, women who love to knit security blankets for sick children. Recently, thousands of these blankets were sent to a refugee camp in Afghanistan to be given to the children."

Karen loved the Charlie Brown cartoon characters so she named her nonprofit organization 'The Linus Project' after Linus, the cartoon character in Snoopy that always carries his security blanket everywhere he goes."

Larry then explained to the four friends, "This story made me realize another important step, the second step in the Charitable Assignment process. Karen did an activity that she enjoyed doing anyway, and was good at, in her case knitting, and used it for the benefit of sick children. She shared her ideas with others through a newspaper story, through her website, and as a result many women across the country do the same thing." Larry also pointed out, "It's important to realize, Karen had other obligations in her life to take care of, but she knit the blankets as she had available time."

Larry continued, "Our second step in the pro-active giving process and in choosing our Charitable Assignment is to decide how much time you can give to your assignment, and after you've decided the time you can give, seek a Charitable Assignment that will be to your liking, and can be done with the time you have available. Don't pick an assignment you will not enjoy."

The four friends were inspired by the story of The Linus Project but it was Tom who spoke up, "The simplicity with which it was started and the almost magical way it expanded and provides benefits to many children is inspiring." Larry added, "It's still growing, The Linus Project is adding chapters, constantly, throughout the country."

Larry then related to the four friends, "Unfortunately most of us, and I did the same thing at the beginning, shy away from taking on a charitable project, shy away from becoming more effective with a charitable activity because we place, in a sense, artificial walls that prevent us from considering it." "What I mean," Larry said, "People will say I don't have time to give, or, I can't afford to give any more money, or they think they don't have the talent, the education or the right contacts. They might say the needs are so great that I couldn't make a difference or there are so many things that I could do, I don't know where to start."

Larry continued, "This is the wrong approach because you're putting the cart before the horse. Before deciding on your Charitable Assignment, before deciding on the specific action to make a difference in more lives, you must first determine what kind of a horse you have. You must first ask yourself, what would I like to focus on - - - and you must ask yourself how much time do I have to give? We all do have time. It may mean that you have to rearrange a few things, but even if you only have one hour a week or a month, or one morning a week or a month, this is the time that you can use for your Charitable Assignment. Ed said, "And everyone has a talent, look at us!" Larry pointed out, "Sure there are people that have more talent than you or I, but each of us have talents in some way, each of us has things that we do well." Tom said, "And, as we heard in Larry's two ex-amples of Aubyn and her brother Welland in the Suitcases for Kids project along with The Linus Project of Karen, money is not the most important part of the Charitable Assignment project." Larry added, "In both of those sto-ries and in so many others, I've learned bring-ing together a focus, giving some of your time and talent, and using collaboration so that other people join with you, will be much more important than the amount of seed money that you provide."

Lunchtime was over, the four friends split the check and happily paid Larry's tab, and of course, left a generous tip for the waitress. Ray said, "So, for our next meeting we will have determine how much time we have to give to our projects." And Tom added, "And we have to reflect on the things that we like to do and the things that we do well so that what-ever time and talents we do have, they will be used to fit our Charitable Assignment."

Larry said, "Terrific, see you next week."

STEP TWO

<u>Your Time and Talent</u>

Do not put - - - the "cart before the horse"

Do not say – I don't have the time to do this

Rather - - - ask how much time you can give

And then – pick a Charitable

Assignment that you can do - - -
With the time that you have to give!

Once again, as the four friends met with Larry at the restaurant, they couldn't believe how fast the time had passed since their last luncheon and they all expressed their excitement, anticipation and appreciation to Larry for introducing these steps to them.

Before they ordered lunch, each of them explained their decision on how much time they could give to the Charitable Assignment. Ray, the retired friend said, "I will be dedicating four hour every Wednesday afternoon." Bob, the teacher, said, "Because of my busy schedule and family obligations I have only one hour per week." Larry explained, "You'll be surprised because you'll find that plenty of time." Tom, the pediatrician said, "I can allocate a half-hour a day by cutting back my lunch break and will use that time thinking of ways I can do my assignment." Finally, Ed, the accountant, said, "I can dedicate two hours per week."

The waitress came and they ordered lunch.

Ed told Larry, "I really appreciate what you told us last week about not putting the cart before the horse, that all we have to do is figure out how much time we could give to our Charitable Assignment and then find an assignment that fits." Ray, Bob and Tom also echoed the same sentiment and said that they all really appreciated this idea of not putting the cart before the horse.

Larry then went on while they were waiting for lunch to be served, "For the third step in the pro-active Charitable Assignment, I've got to tell you a moving story about another charitable hero that I recently read about. Rita Schiavone had been a stay-at-home mom with her three children for many years but now that they were grown up, she had free time and planned to return to college to earn her degree, but also wanted to help people in need. She asked a friend of hers, the director at the local YMCA for ideas and he gave Rita the name of an elderly woman by the name of Minnie who he knew had very little family and was lonely. When Rita called on Minnie for the first time she was appalled at the small amount of food in the refrigerator. Rita learned that not only was Minnie elderly, but was practically blind and living with her daughter who was physically and mentally handicapped. As she chatted with Minnie she discovered that because she had no other children or relatives in the area she had very few visitors and was very lonely and was eating very poorly." Ed commented, "Minnie was sure lucky to have Rita for company."

Larry continued, "That evening when Rita was fixing supper for herself and her husband she decided to prepare an extra plate for Minnie, froze that extra meal and the next day brought it to Minnie, heated it in the microwave oven, and then visited with her for about an hour." Tom asked, "Did she do that every night?" Larry replied, "No, Rita didn't put the cart before the horse, she decided she had enough time for a weekly visit with Minnie. Rita later said, 'I truly received more from my visits than I ever gave to Minnie.'"

Larry went on, "One day Rita shared her story with her pastor who then shared the idea with members of the congregation. Several members of the church liked the idea so much that they started doing the same thing. Preparing a meal, as an extra plate at dinner, freezing the meal, and then bringing it to a lonely elderly person for a weekly visit.

Bob observed, "Such a simple yet compassionate idea." Larry said, "Rita started this several years ago, but do you know that today in the Philadelphia area there are over 800,000 meals served exactly this way, with home visits to lonely elderly citizens?" Bob continued, "It's amazing how these people in your stories see a need, don't get weighed down by the size of the task, they just do what they can about that one need, helping one or a few children or adults."

Larry said, "It is amazing, but what I discovered through this story was the third essential step in a pro-active giving Charitable Assignment. That step is Collaboration. Simply doing whatever you can do to inspire others to act in a similar way or to join you in your particular mission. Rita simply shared her story, a simple idea, a weekly visit to Minnie, and she was the spark that inspired many other people, starting with her own church members, to do likewise." Ed said, "I see the importance of collaboration. By Rita sharing her story many more lonely elderly people were helped."

Larry then said, "Remember the story of Aubyn Burnside and the suitcases she provided for foster children and how she, through telling her story, inspired many other children to establish chapters in all of the 50 states. Remember the story of Karen Loukes who established The Linus Project, who once again, simply made her story available inspiring women who loved to knit, across the entire the country, to knit blankets for sick children."

Tom said, "I'm really inspired by this, these simple assignments, started by ordinary people and how they grew to such a large extent." He said, "It seems too simple and easy, and certainly an idea that we have missed in our approach to charitable giving." Ed said, "Now I know Larry how you were able to accomplish so many things and help so many children that you told me about. All the time I thought it was about just giving more and more money. Now I understand that it's principally about giving some of your time, some of talent, and then using the magical and explosive power of collaboration."

The friends all took a break as the waitress came and served their meals and used the time to eat and briefly reflect on Larry's third step - this magic of collaboration.

Tom said to Larry, "I know what our assignment is for this next week." "Sure," Ed chimed in, "Our assignment is to think of ways in which we could use collaboration, that is, how to get others to join with us, taking into consideration what we have decided to focus on, taking into consideration the time we're going to give to our Charitable Assignment and then next week review our ideas with each other."

Larry said, "Don't try to change the whole world or the whole country. Just concentrate on sharing your idea with others, family, friends, co-workers, church members, a social group or an employer. Invite others to join with you, or to follow your example, if they wish. Remember, in each of the stories that we talked about before, these were ordinary people, they weren't wealthy, they did not have advance degrees or special contacts, they simply reached out to help one, sometimes a few children or adults in a way that they could – using some of their time and talent and then they simply shared their story with others."

STEP THREE

Collaboration

You can always – always – always
Accomplish a lot more
If you invite and inspire others - - - to
join with you!

Two persons can always accomplish
more than just one!

The next Wednesday was cloudy, dreary and rainy. The sun was not to be seen, but, as the four friends, along with Larry gathered for their weekly luncheon, their excitement was evident. They were beginning to really get into the swing - into the spirit of this new approach to charitable giving and beginning to anticipate how they would enjoy the process and what they could accomplish.

The waitress came over, took their orders and then brought them their coffee, water and sodas.

Ray said, "Isn't it amazing how animated the four of us are at these meetings. I never knew charitable giving could be this interesting. When Larry arrived he could see the anticipation and said, "Gentleman, I can tell you're eager to share how collaboration was integrated into your Charitable Assignment. Why don't we just jump right in?"   Ray started by saying, "I'm a member of a very active retired persons club that meets weekly and has about 150 members and I know that some of the members will join me to help."

Bob stated, "The group that I will be able to ask for collaboration is the teachers' union group in the Town of Plainville. I'm pretty certain I could find help there."

Tom, our pediatrician, said "I have contact with mothers every single day as they bring their children in for exams and treatments, I'll try to enlist the help of mothers to collaborate with me and hopefully be inspired by my actions."

Ed, our accountant, explained, "I feel I have two possible sources of collaboration. First, I work for a company where there are 200 employees and some of my co-workers will be inspired to join with me, and I also belong to the local association of certified public accountants that meets monthly, and this will also be a source of collaboration for me."

It took only a few minutes for each of them to explain their decision on collaboration. Larry reminded them, "You should write this down as you go through the various steps." Each of them in unison said they already had. "Wonderful." Larry exclaimed. They were anxious to listen to Larry as he explained the fourth step in this new pro-active giving approach.

Larry started by saying that, "You know, in this country, if you mention charitable giving to any person they immediately think of writing a check. Writing a check seems to be the primary and sometimes the only steps that are taken by most people in their charitable giving. I'm sure you've discovered by now that we've turned the tables on that so that our fourth step when we talk about money in our different approach, our pro-active giving approach, the amount of money is the least important of the four steps."

Ray said, "I suppose you're going to tell us another inspiring story? I must admit, that's what they do – inspire."

Larry replied, "Yes I am. To explain this fourth step which is entitled 'Seed Money' before I tell you our new story, I'd like to remind you of the three prior examples - Aubyn started the collection of suitcases, Karen started with the knitting of blankets for sick children, and Rita started by just visiting Minnie and bringing her companionship and a healthy meal. The striking thing of these three stories, which have all been the sparks to create outstanding charitable organizations, the amount of money was not important." Ed said, "They all were simple acts of kindness."

Larry then continued, "Let me tell you the story of Miles Postlewait, a 10 year old boy who was born with some congenital heart defects who was in the hospital for an operation to correct his condition. This was not the only time that Miles had to spend time in the hospital, and one day, in his innocence, he said to his mother, 'I really wish that I could have a friend, a buddy, just like me who would share with me all of these things that I have to go through because of my illness.' Out of the innocence of that remark his mother contacted a local seamstress and asked her to create a doll with a hospital gown and under the hospital gown put a small pouch with a zipper and the impression of a heart. When the doll was ready Miles' mother gave it to Miles and said 'Let this be your Shadow Buddy, a doll that you can take with you through all of your hospital stays. If you look under his hospital gown you'll see that he has a heart just like yours that needs some minor repairs, he'll go with you to the operating room, if you need to take a pill, he will take one with you and when the doctor comes in to explain what they're going to do to make you better, he'll explain it to you and your Shadow Buddy together." Ray asked, "Did it help Miles?"

Larry answered, "It made such a difference to Miles during his hospital stay and was such a source of comfort to him that after Miles was better and released from the hospital his mother contacted a local doll maker to construct similar dolls for other sick children. She shared the idea with a local service club who gladly sponsored the purchase of a supply of these dolls and distributed them to the hospital for sick children. Tom asked, "Did this idea spread across the country too?" Larry smiled and answered, "As a matter of fact it did. 'Shadow Buddy Dolls' are being used in over 60 hospitals throughout the country. They're constructed with different medical conditions and they're used extensively by doctors to explain to the child the procedures that he or she will be going through. If an IV is needed, one is given to the Shadow Buddy. Any medical steps that the child has to experience are also experienced by his or her Shadow Buddy. Service groups all over the country purchase these dolls to distribute them to hospitals so that they could be given to children to ease their anxiety during their hospital stays."

Ed pointed out, "Just like the other stories, you can see that the Seed Money that was involved in this Shadow Buddy project was only the cost of the initial doll."

Bob said, "So my understanding is that our next assignment before next Wednesday is to decide how much seed money each of us is willing to put in." Larry said, "That's exactly correct Bob, and remember, when you do your Charitable Assignment you'll have 90 days to do it, and please remember these four stories that so strikingly illustrate that it's only seed money that's needed."

The waitress came over with their meals, the friends ate and shared additional ideas then put on their hats and coats, opened their umbrellas and left.

STEP FOUR

Seed Money

With pro-active giving you only need
 "Seed Money"
          And money is the least
important of the four steps in your
- - - pro-active giving Charitable
Assignment.

The next Wednesday, in contrast to last week, was a beautiful day. The sun was shining, there was a gentle breeze and it was one of those days that really made you feel good to be alive.

As the friends joined for lunch, you could see and feel their anticipation and their anxiousness to get started with their Charitable Assignment.

After coffees and waters were delivered by the waitress and the lunch had been ordered, Ray started out by saying, "I decided that I would provide seed money of $250 for my assignment." Bob said, "I decided I will donate $200." Tom said, "I think $150 of seed money will work." Ed said, "I will put in $100 of my money as seed money."

Tom said, "This doesn't seem like much money." But Larry quickly reminded him and the other friends "The seed money is the least important step in this new approach to charitable giving." Tom said to Larry, "I want to express my real appreciation to you for sharing these great ideas with us. I know I speak for all of us when I say that I'm really anxious to start my charitable project and see what kind of a difference I can make." Ed said to Larry, "Do you have any closing thoughts for us, suggestions or anything you can add to the excellent ideas you've already shared with us?" Larry responded, "I sure have. Stay with the four steps in your Charitable Assignment and remember to keep in mind your focus, to give some of your time and talent, and think of ways to be most effective. Always be aware of and seeking out ways to use collaboration to have other people join with you to be more effective and to remember to use the money you contribute as true seed money to see how they can make it grow."

Larry also reminded them to allow 90 days, more or less, to do their assignments. He also said, "Take your time, don't try to change the world, but simply try to change one life or a few lives". You will find, as I found, you'll be absolutely amazed with what will be accomplished by you through diligently following these four steps. It's really important to make sure it's an enjoyable process, not a burden or an obligation. Do things that fit within your talent and your own personality so that the entire Charitable Assignment becomes and is truly a rewarding experience for you. Ed said, "It sounds like if we figure out a match for our available time, use our talents and apply focus and collaboration it will be more enjoyable." Larry said, "Yes, exactly, and as time goes on and as you finish your assignments, you will discover, as I have, that you truly can make a difference in the world, that you can help other people and change their lives and, more importantly, that your own life will change each day for the better in one small way and you will come to experience the truth of the statement that it is truly better to give than to receive."

Larry then said, "Before our meals arrive let's take a few minutes for each of you to summarize how you're going to apply the four steps in doing your own pro-active Charitable Assignment."

Ray our retired purchasing agent said, "I've decided to:

Focus – on one homeless family.

Time - four hours a week every Wednesday afternoon.

Collaboration – retired persons from my club.

Seed Money – will be $250."

Bob, the teacher of the sixth grade said, "I've figured out I'll use my:

Focus – to help a child or a few children living in poverty in our town.

Time – one hour per week.

Collaboration – teachers' union and association.

Seed Money - $200."

Tom, our local pediatrician said, "I will use:

Focus – to help children enhance their education.

Time – two and a half hours per week

Collaboration – mothers of children who are my patients.

Seed Money - $150."

Ed, the accountant said:

"Focus – education of children.

Time – two hours per week.

Collaboration – co-workers and other accountants in the local CPA association.

Seed Money - $100."

The waitress brought their meals and they continued to share ideas and insights as they ate, had coffee and dessert.

Before we leave, Larry said, "I know you'll continue your weekly meetings as you have for the last several years and that you'll continue to share your experiences with your Charitable Assignments and I know that each one of you will be helpful to each other by sharing your insights and you will start to feel the enthusiasm and see the good results you're accomplishing."

Larry then said, "If you don't mind I would like to join you in three months?" Of course everyone agreed. "So let's mark our calendars and set the date now. At this luncheon I will simply be a listener and each of you will explain how your Charitable Assignment was carried out, what you accomplished, who was helped and how you started the process of collaboration along with the effect this project had on you, personally."

Each of the four friends couldn't thank Larry enough for sharing his ideas, his insights, and for introducing them to this new way to approach charitable giving in their own lives. "See you in 90 days," said Larry as he left the restaurant.

During the next three months the four friends continued to meet as they had every Wednesday for the last several years. While in past luncheons they talked about many different things, it seemed like the focus of their meetings always came back to what they were doing with their Charitable Assignments. You could see and feel the enthusiasm and the excitement that each one of them was experiencing in expressing new thoughts and new ideas and new methods to reach out to help children and families in the community. They shared ideas each week with one another on how they were progressing and the good feelings they were experiencing from this pro-active approach to charitable giving.

At one meeting Ed said, "I always used to feel that I wasn't doing enough when I wrote checks to different charities. But now, by giving some of my time and talent and seeing how my money is being used to make a difference, I feel that I'm really contributing to help other people." Tom said, "I feel the same way and I'm beginning to realize more and more that to really make a difference you have to put some of yourself into your charitable giving and you have to focus on something that has meaning to you, and you have to use the

talents and resources that you have." Ed added, "I realize now that it's not primarily about
money, but more about giving in a pro-active,
positive, effective way."

Bob said, "I can hardly wait until we meet
with Larry again to go over with him all that
we've accomplished because of his insights
and ideas that he shared with us."

It was a perfect day when the four friends
gathered at the restaurant in the middle of
June. This luncheon was special because
the three-month period had passed and each
of them had completed their Charitable
Assignments. Bob, the teacher, remarked,
"We're acting like the young boys in my class
– we can't wait to report to Larry what we
accomplished. Tom said, "It is amazing how
much of an impact we had on the community and what a real difference it made in our
own lives." Larry arrived a few minutes later
and was warmly greeted by the four friends.
After they have ordered their drinks, Larry
said, "I've been anticipating this meeting and
looking forward to it. While I had done a lot
of talking at our prior meetings to explain my
ideas, at this meeting I'm really going to be a
listener and let the four of you explain what
you've accomplished."

Ray said, "I'd be glad to go first and tell you what I've done and just how great it made me, my wife, our children, and the volunteers feel.

Since I had decided to focus on helping one homeless family with $250 of seed money along with four hours per week, I started by spending quite a bit of time during the first two Wednesdays reading about homelessness in America, in our state, and even in our own community. I was shocked to read that in America today, with all its affluence, there are over one million children that are homeless each night. There are homeless children in our own communities and in fact in the City of Capitalville, just 20 miles from us, a city of about 100,000 people, there are between 200 and 300 homeless children each and every night." Ed said, "Those are powerful yet sad statistics."

Ray went on, "I was also shocked to read that because of the lack of affordable hous-ing that many times families spend three to six months, sometimes even more in a shelter before having the opportunity to leave. Many homeless families are working poor families where parents do work but their wages are so low or the cost of living is so high, or a parent may have lost a job because of downsizing, because of sickness, and these families are often just one paycheck away from homelessness. I was really glad that I had decided that my Charitable Assignment would be to help a homeless family, locally."

Ray continued, "I visited a local shelter and talked to the director explaining my motivation and asked him if he would designate a willing homeless family that I could help in some way. He introduced me to Ramon and Maria who had moved here from Puerto Rico several years ago and have two children, ages 5 and 7. They had little chance for education, did not finish high school but were good parents and real hard workers. Ramon had been on the maintenance crew of a local company, which, when it downsized and moved most of its operation to another state, he was laid-off. Maria worked as a housekeeper for a few hours each day because she still had the two children and all of her housekeeping duties. They hadn't been able to save money at all and lived in an apartment that was very expensive for them, always struggling to get by. Bob said, "Imagine working that hard and all those worries." Ray said, "And of course Ramon continued to look for new employment, which

was difficult because of his limited experience, his limited language, and to make matters worse, there was a fire in the apartment
building where they lived and all of the tene-
ments were severely damaged and most of
their furnishings were lost in the fire. That's
when they entered the shelter with a bleak out-
look for the future. They had been in the shelter for about 5 weeks when I met them."

Tom asked, "Could their luck be any
worse?" Ray responded, "I decided to try to
enlist the help of some of the members in my
retired men's club for collaboration. The first
job of course was for us to try to help them
find an apartment so I shared my concern and
my assignment with the club members. Eight
of them immediately signed on to help and to
join with me in looking for an apartment."

Ray continued, "We really rolled up our
sleeves and committed ourselves to spending
our Wednesday afternoons together pouring
over the apartment listings in the newspapers,
contacted agencies and landlords we knew,
members of our different church groups and
in about two weeks we were fortunate enough
to find an owner of a two family house with a
small apartment that they had not rented for
several years. We visited the apartment and

while it was small it would be adequate for
their needs. It needed a lot of sprucing up,
but once again, we rolled up our sleeves and
starting on the very next Wednesday with four
more members of the club who joined with us
for a very effective crew to first thoroughly
clean the apartment and then on the following two Wednesdays we painted the entire
apartment." Ed said, "You had great success
with your collaboration." Ray pointed out,
"I was very fortunate because when we finished it was clean as a whistle and bright and
cheery. You could imagine the joy of Ramon
and Marie and their two children when they
learned we had found an apartment for them
and had not only had we cleaned it from top to
bottom but we also did the painting, they were
thrilled. By the way, I used $150 of my $250
to purchase some of the paint for the apartment, a couple of the other members contributed money to purchase the rest of the paint
that we needed. My wife and three wives of
the other group members then set to work in
purchasing and hanging new curtains for all
of the windows.

The group's next job was to find some way
to furnish the apartment because they had
lost just about everything in the fire. We pre-

pared a list of what was needed – furniture, pictures, small appliances, personal items. Tom interjected, "You needed just about everything." Ray answered, "Yes we did. We took the list and went back to the retired men's club with another appeal and it was surprising how many men responded with furniture, small appliances, which many of them purchased to furnish the apartment. A few of us even visited three of the local furniture stores, explained our plight and what we were trying to do and each of the furniture stores donated at least one, and in one case four pieces of furniture for their apartment. We furnished and decorated an entire apartment, complete with new curtains and pictures hung by our wives. By then about two months had gone by in my Charitable Assignment time period and I felt we had accomplished much more than I ever thought we would." Ed said, "Truly amazing work Ray." Ray responded, "Yes, but we had one additional problem that had to be met. We had to join together to see if we could find Ramon a job that he could make a decent wage at, a job that he would be proud to work at, and one where he'd get good health benefits and other benefits for his family. By this time I had a core group of a dozen men who agreed to spend Wednesday afternoons with me for the next three or four weeks to focus on this job search. We combed the Want Ads, we asked the other members of the retirement club if they had any contacts with companies and we asked for suggestions and ideas. We called resource directors at local companies and we all pitched in. During the fourth Wednesday we struck pay dirt. An established company had just lost one of their key people in the shipping department. The time was right, the job was perfect for Ramon and the manager of the shipping department and the president of the company both welcomed him with open arms."

Ray continued, "By this time we had just one Wednesday left to devote to our Charitable Assignment and we decided that we would take Ramon, Maria and their two children along with our wives out for a special dinner of celebration. We all felt so proud of what we had accomplished, the dinner was an event that I will never forget. The bonds of friendship were strengthened between the club members and their wives who participated in the Charitable Assignment and a close bond of friendship was formed between all of us and

Ramon, Maria and their children and it will last a lifetime."

Tom said, "What a wonderful experience." Then Ray said, "I can't remember when I participated in something that was as satisfying as this. I still get a lump in my throat from merely telling you what we accomplished - even my own children told me how proud they were of what we had accomplished, and, oh, by the way, I still had $50 left from my Seed Money, which I simply gave to the family.

I now can truly appreciate what Larry explained to us and can confirm 100% with him that it is truly better to give than to receive."

Next, Tom, the pediatrician was anxious to explain and relate to his friends and Larry what he had accomplished by doing his Charitable Assignment. "As you know," Tom said, "I decided that I would focus on helping children to in someway enhance their education. I felt that I was helping children physically by keeping them healthy and helping them recover from illnesses, but I could also help them in another way to improve their education."

Tom went on, "First I had to decide exactly what I should do. I started by going to the Sarah's Bookstore and the library looking for information on ways that I might improve the education of the children that were my patients. In addition to that, three of the mothers whose children are patients of mine are teachers, mostly in the elementary grades, and I called them and asked if I could meet with them. Each of them was very enthusiastic and happy to come to the office and spend some time with me helping me to find a way to increase and enhance the education of children.

What I found out from my reading and particularly from the teachers really surprised me. They said that close to 40% of the children entering the early grades needed help with remedial reading. They also told me that the ability of a child to read, to understand what he or she is reading, and to develop at an early age a love of reading, was the most important thing that could be done or achieved in the early education of each child."

Tom continued, "This really shocked me. While I know our community is not affluent and I know we have working poor families, by and large we have a moderately wealthy community. I wondered why many children entered school with this handicap. I learned from the three teachers and the reading that I did - in this busy world many times with both parents working there simply doesn't seem to be enough time to put aside for this. The teachers also told me that they didn't feel that mothers and fathers really and truly appreciated the importance of reading to children, especially in the early years.

It struck me like a lightening bolt, that this is what I could do. Promote the importance of good reading skills in children. After all, my career and the fact that I see children and mothers each and every day would lend itself very easily to this mission and purpose.

I started printing the information I'd read including the comments of the teachers about the importance of reading being the one single thing that parents could do to help their children in their education. I carefully arranged the information so that it was easy to read, brought it Charlie's Print Shop and arranged for him to print it on a colorful brochure and decided to give one of these brochures to each of the mothers who came into my office.

I started the next day by spending a few minutes at the end of each appointment talking to the mother, in the presence of the child, about the extreme importance of reading and that in our busy society the importance of doing this one thing would enhance the education of their children. I asked them to share this information with their husband and also with other children who might be old enough to read to other children in the family and to set aside at least one hour a day for this purpose. I convinced them that just this one simple thing would bring great rewards in the education of their children and convinced them that it was something they should start to do immediately."

Bob asked, "So you got a positive response?" Tom answered, "All of the mothers thanked me, some of them emphatically for sharing this information with them. A couple of them told me how proud they were of me that I was going beyond the physical wellbeing of their children and doing something to help in their education. Why just the other day, Mary, one of our young mothers gave me a bear hug and told me how she appreciated this information and that she would start reading with her child that very night.

I can't begin to describe the joy that this one idea that I'm putting into practice with my patients and the happiness it brings to me every single day. I see the expression of appreciation in the eyes of the parents, in what they say to me, and how much they appreciate

the information that I've given them. I show-
case the brochures in my waiting room so that
if a mother has to wait she's invited to read it
and I make sure that she has the information
to bring home.

In recent weeks I've been thinking about
ways that I could expand this idea. I already
know that I'm going to continue this program
for as long as I have my own practice. It's so
rewarding, I feel that I'm affecting the lives
of all of my patients and it just makes me feel
terribly good.

"Did you come up with an expansion
plan?" asked Ray. Tom responded, "Yes, I
decided to start accumulating gently owned
children's books that families have outgrown
so as I explain the importance to every mother
and child that comes into the office I'll be able
to give to that child a book for him or her to
take home with each and every visit. I don't
feel I'll have to buy the books because I will
create and distribute a flyer asking mothers to
make donations of books that their children
have outgrown. I may take the idea to the local bookstores and perhaps to the library to
collect good quality pre-owned books.

Just last week two things happened that
show great promise for expanding this idea.

I'm sure most of you know Sam Mason, the pediatrician. Sam and I are very good friends and we often consult with one another over medical problems of children. Sam found out what I was doing, invited me for lunch last week and asked me to explain. Sam was impressed and said that he was going to implement the same idea immediately in his office. As I left lunch that day I said to myself, just think, with Sam instituting the same program in his office will double the effect of this." Ray pointed out, "Tom, that's terrific, you already expanded your program in two ways. One by furnishing gently used books to parents to read with their children and you enlisted a fellow pediatrician to do the same." "And," Tom continued, "one day a couple of weeks ago, one of the mothers that I talked to is a part-time reporter for the Daily Eagle. She asked if I would be willing to have a story written about what I was doing and particularly about how important reading is in the education of each and every child. I told Theresa I would be willing to tell my story but I asked her to wait another 5-6 months so that I could have the complete program in place and through follow-up visits from the mothers to discuss their comments and suggestions.

Theresa agreed, although I decided when the story does appear in the paper I do not want credit. I want the story to focus on the importance of this reading program and hopefully this will inspire others to do the same thing.

When I spoke with Theresa about the program, Larry, it reminded me of the examples that you'd given us and how mere publicity caused Suitcases for Kids and The Linus Project to expand greatly.

I can't tell you how much joy and satisfaction this Charitable Assignment has given to me and will continue to give to me during all of my practice. I can't thank you enough, Larry, for introducing this idea to me because it has made such a difference in my charitable practice. I can't believe I still have a little over $100 of my seed money that I haven't even spent yet."

Bob was the next one to tell his story and the excitement over what he had accomplished was evident. "As you fellows know I've been a teacher in sixth grade for many years and I really enjoy working with the kids. I put up $200 as seed money, decided that I would in some way help a child or some children in the community who did not have much and that I would provide one hour per week to work on my assignment. For collaboration I would look to other teachers who are friends of mine and teachers in the association.

As Larry had suggested and as Tom explained, I also took the good part of a month to think about different things that I could do." Ed commented, "That's time well spent." Bob continued, "Two events that happened to me or that I observed made it easy for me to make my decision. First, I recalled that last Christmas at my church they established a giving tree where each of us could take the name of a child in the community who might not have much for Christmas and buy that child a gift. Sometime in the month of February I happened to be visiting my daughter and two of my grandchildren and when I went down the cellar to help my son-in-law move a piece of furniture, I noticed quite a few toys on shelves and in corners of the cellar. I asked my daughter about them and she said, 'These are all toys that our children have outgrown and I really don't want to throw them away but I don't really know who to give them to.'

That single statement got me thinking. At Christmas time it seems all of us, or at least hundreds of us come out to buy toys for children who might have less than our children or grandchildren have. I asked myself what about these same children the rest of the year? What about them at their birthdays, aren't they entitled have some of the magic of Christmas given to them throughout the year? And then it struck me, why don't I take the good quality, gently used toys that my grandchildren have outgrown and arrange to give them to children who don't have anywhere near as much." Ray said, "It sure pays to be observant." Bob went on, "I shared this idea with a few of the teachers and even at the next meeting of the Teachers' Association and received a great deal of support from a lot of the teachers who offered to participate.

I then took about an hour to prepare a simple flyer which I sent home with each of my students in the sixth grade. I explained with them what I was doing, sent the flyer home with them so that their parents could read about it and asked them if they had toys that were still in good shape that they had outgrown that they bring them to school during the next 30 days and we would put them together and redistribute them to other children. When I talked about this idea with a few of my friends who are also teachers, three of them immediately decided that they would like to do exactly the same thing in their classes, which they did."

Ed pointed out, "So at that point; you had the four steps ready to implement." Bob answered, "Yes I did. We all agreed to the 30 day limit to accumulate the toys and to give ourselves time to look them over, be sure they were safe and clean before we distributed them. As the toys were being accumulated I contacted several local social agencies, told them what I was doing and asked their advice." Tom asked, "Did you find them helpful because I know they can be very busy." Bob responded, "It took a few phone calls but eventually I received enthusiastic responses from several social workers who said they dealt with several families where the children had very little and that their lives would be enriched by the distribution of these good quality, pre-owned toys.

You can imagine my surprise when with just four classes and a simple request we collected over 300 toys including games, puzzles, good quality action toys, a wonderful supply of excellent stuffed animals for children from birth to age three, and a small collection of dolls and trucks. We even received a beautiful dollhouse with a full supply of furniture, a child's kitchen sink, stove, with a grill and artificial hamburgers and other food items, all of which proved to be in excellent condition.

My wife and two of my adult children, together with the other three teachers that participated in the project, then checked each of the toys for safety and cleanliness.

At the Red Cross we donated 25 beautiful stuffed animals which they explained they would give out to children who may experience a fire or other casualty. We brought another 25 stuffed animals to the shelter for battered women who again explained that this would help soften the blow for children who had to stay in the shelter. One of the other agencies that helps young single mothers took over 100 articles, many of them action toys for young children, a supply of stuffed animals, and many baby toys and articles. We were assured everything would be very well received. Another agency dealing with families took the rest of our items and would distribute them to a multitude of families in the next month or two after receiving them.

We received thank you notes not only from the agencies and from the social workers, but also from many families. They described the joy of their children who received the toys.

As we read these thank you notes I can't explain the sense of satisfaction and the good feelings each of us had. Several of the notes from the children themselves brought tears to our eyes. It was then when I truly appreciated what Larry had explained to us - that we really got back a heck of a lot more than we gave. The project was so easy that the four of us, that is myself and the other three teachers who participated said we really ought to do this on a regular or at least on an annual basis. Tom said, "What a terrific idea." Bob continued, "I thought it couldn't get any better and then we started getting a lot of notes from mothers who donated toys telling us how much they appreciated the chance to see that their toys were being given to other children rather than simply collecting dust in their cellars or garages. You know Larry, when you first explained this idea to us while it sounded exciting I still had my doubts. Those doubts are gone and I really appreciate the truth of everything you explained to us and truly appreciate your taking the time to do this. I found in my life a new way to give. The pro-active Charitable

Assignment approach brings tremendous
benefits and really helps other people. I can
see the results of my efforts, it's easy to do,
I don't have to change my lifestyle and the
emphasis is not on money but just providing
a small amount of seed money. By the way,
of the $200 I provided I only spent about $60
so far for bags to deliver the toys in, the cost
of printing flyers and some other miscella-
neous expenses. I still have the remainder of
my seed money to do another toys for kids
project. And as luck would have it, a sister
of one of the teachers writes for the Plainville
Evening News and I expect we'll probably
have an article very soon on the toys for kids
project which we hope will encourage other
parents to consider giving their toys to children in the area.

Larry, thanks a lot for explaining this idea
to us and guiding us through it. It truly is a
life-changing event."

Ed, the accountant, was the last of the four
friends to explain what he had done as his assignment. Ed said, "As far as you fellows remember I decided that I would do something
with the talents I have to help in someway
with the education of children - to enhance
their education. I had agreed that I would

spend at least two hours a week thinking and planning for the way to do this and planned on $100 of seed money.

Like Tom, I spent well over a month just thinking of ways that I might be able to help children in the community to enhance their education. I talked to teachers, I talked to friends of mine who are also accountants and I just continued to look for ideas during this first month." Bob asked, "So what did you come up with?" Ed replied, "Well, I remembered last year when I took part in career day at Plainville High. I spoke for 30 minutes about the profession of accounting and was one of a number of different professionals that did the same thing. As I put myself in the shoes of the students, I kind of said to myself, 'Would this really give me an understanding of what the accounting profession was about, what it does and why it's important?' I had to answer no to that question because I felt that what the students needed were hands-on examples of what accountants did to illustrate why what they do is important. I also felt these examples should be in a format the student could relate to and demonstrate how the accounting profession has everyday useful purposes.

I began by sharing this idea with three friends who were part of the local Certified Public Accountants' Association. One of them suggested that I go into one class and work with the students over a morning or afternoon with a case study showing what we do and why it's important to a business. The three associates said they'd like to collaborate with me and would be willing to visit with a class of students. We arranged to meet the next week for a few hours to outline an example we could use with the students. I contacted my sister-in-law who is a ninth grade teacher and made arrangements with her and three of her fellow teachers for us to all come in on a specific day and work with the students."

Tom asked, "Did that take a lot of time?" Ed responded, "No, because when my associates and I met the next week we put our heads together and worked out a very simple problem a small business owner could have. The business sells three different products and we worked out a simple profit and loss statement that showed a net profit for the business for the last two years. We decided what we would illustrate to the students that while a net profit was being made by the business we decided to show them, through a hands-on example, that two of the products were profitable but the third was not and that the unprofitable product was simply reducing the profit that could be made by the other two products. We worked out the details, placed all of the numbers on a simple profit and loss statement and I arranged to get copies printed so that the teachers could give the students the example in advance. The example simply showed various costs and expenses, some of them general, some of them related to specific products.

The following month the four of us went into the classrooms and spent an entire morning working with the students to explain how accountants can segregate the specific profits and losses for specific products and why this is extremely important to each business no matter how large or how small. We didn't just explain the statement, we had the students join us while reviewing the profit and loss statement, and making it a working illustration and asking them to allocate costs to specific products, and when calculating the net profit of each product separately they saw that the profit of the business was substantially increased when we deleted the product line that was not producing a profit."

I can tell you that this was one of the best mornings I'd spent in the last year. The kids eyes were opened, it really gave me a lot of pleasure to work with them because it was clear they now understood what accountants do in our business relationships and why we are important to every business no matter how small or how large. I know the kids enjoyed the morning tremendously because they expressed their appreciation. I'm convinced this is a much better way to introduce careers rather than just a 30 minute speech.

The three associates expressed the same satisfaction with what we'd done and they all said this was one of the most enjoyable mornings that they'd spent for as long as they could remember. We all felt that we were giving something back and enhancing the education of the children. As a matter of fact, we enjoyed ourselves so much that we're planning to do this on a regular basis in the schools and plan to tell our story at the next meeting of the local accountants' association which has 75 members in it. I'm positive that other members are going to want to join us. Why, just last week one of my three associates who took part in this program who is also on the board of directors of the statewide Certified

Public Accountants' Association explained the idea to the other statewide directors and they showed a great interest in this concept. My friend indicated to me that he feels that perhaps the state association may get involved and sponsor this kind of an annual career day where accountants all over the state enter schools to do something similar. This made me really feel good because I was not only enlarging my Charitable Assignment but the thought that perhaps it will, in the near future, become a statewide effort.

I definitely have found a new way to give back to children using the talents that I have and can agree with Tom, Bob and Ray that I really got back a lot more than I gave here. I've only used about $50 of the $100 seed money that I had put aside, mostly for printing costs and supplies that we used for the students."

I also want to join in with the rest of you in thanking you, Larry, very sincerely, for bringing this idea to us and coaching us on the very simple, yet powerful and effective way to enjoy charitable giving through a pro-active Charitable Assignment. I never stopped to consider how much good I could do to help in the education of children by doing something that was totally enjoyable to me, using the accounting talents that I have. It really surprised me that I got back more than I gave."

Tom said to Larry, "I know that I speak for all us when I say that we can't thank you enough for taking the time to bring to us these ideas and sharing this approach to charitable giving which has really opened my eyes and the eyes of all of us. For many years I've felt I couldn't make a difference so I kind of did nothing. I always felt that my life was so busy that I couldn't possibly give any time to helping others, but by sharing your insights and your stories with us Larry you opened our eyes to the simple direct things that we could do that really could make a difference in the lives of other people especially when you think in terms of only one life at a time." Larry said to all of them, "I really appreciated the chance to meet with you and I'd like to stop in again from time to time at your meetings and see how things are going and see how your Charitable Assignments are doing and whether they increased, which I know they will, or whether you've taken on new assignments." Bob said, "I know I speak for all of us Larry when we say you're always welcome, we really enjoyed meeting you, having you for one of our friends, and I for one will be indebted to you for a lifetime for giving me this new approach to charitable giving." The waitress came brought their meals and they finished them exchanging pleasantries.

As they were wrapping up their meals Larry said to the four friends, "And now before we end this lunch I'd like to ask each of you to do a favor for me." Ed said, "I know we all would be glad to help in anyway we can." Larry answered, "I would like you to take the time to share this approach to charitable giving with other people. You can start with the members of your family, your spouse, or your children, share your ideas with co-workers and friends, siblings. I believe that as more and more people adopt this approach to their charitable giving that we can really, in time, change the world."

Larry continued, "Before we go, I also want to express my thanks to each of you. As I shared these ideas with you and saw that each of you accomplished great things by carrying out your own pro-active Charitable Assignments, I can't describe to you the amount of joy it brings to me. See, whenever you make something happen that makes a difference in the lives of other people, what will come back to you will be much more than you have given."

A Message from the Author

"We make a living by what we get
We make a life by what we give."
Winston Churchill, Statesmen

A Purpose for Your Life

It has been written that millions of Americans are searching for some meaning to their lives, and are asking themselves, what is the purpose of my life? What am I here for?

Many Americans today are discovering that there should be more to life than just the greater accumulation of material goods – that there must be some meaning to life beyond the increased pursuit of recreational activities or simply living the "good life" as it is called.

Sometime ago I read a remarkable classic book by Viktor E. Frankl, a brilliant and talented author and professor who spent several years in concentration camps during the Second World War. His book, "Man's Search

for Meaning" explains what he discovered
and it describes in detail life in the concentration camps. He tell us that the persons who
survived the camps and its atrocities were the
persons such as himself who had a purpose
or a meaning in life that they had to return to,
someone or something that they had to get back
to or to accomplish. In Professor Frankl's case
he had written an entire book on man's search
for meaning in life and had his only manuscript
with him on a train when he was seized and
placed in the concentration camp. His motivation to survive and to re-write the book what
was what carried him through and he noticed
all of the other prisoners that survived had
some strong and powerful motive to survive the
camp and to accomplish something.

A few years ago a book called "The
Purpose Driven Life" by Rick Warren reached
the bestseller list on a national basis within
a short time of its publication and continued
on the bestseller list for a long time. It stated
the fact that each one of us has to find within
ourselves some purpose or meaning for our
lives. The wide and immediate popularity
of this book illustrated the thirst of so many
American people to find a meaning and purpose for their own lives.

It is my hope that you too will try this new simple approach to charitable giving in your own life. By following the four simple steps explained by Larry, you will find that you will change two lives, the life of the child, the family or the individual that you help and your own life. You will find that as you help others, you will help yourself even more by finding a new purpose and a new meaning in your own life.

The Acorn and the Oak Tree

Each day we see beautiful oak trees in our yards, along our streets, in our woods. It is easy to forget that these great oak trees, in the beginning, were tiny acorns.

Although the time, the effort and the amount of money you spend in the beginning may seem small, just like the tiny acorn, you can be the seed for change in the community – in the nation – in the world.

Will you plant an acorn?

Putting the Cart Before the Horse

Despite the fact that America has reached its greatest time of affluence, there are millions of children that are homeless each night, live in poverty, have inadequate education, are abused or are subject to violence and forced to live in foster homes. We read about working families that cannot afford adequate health insurance. It is normal to feel as we read about the enormity of these problems that we really can't make a difference.

We put the cart before the horse. We feel that we don't have enough time or enough money or enough talent or enough contacts to really make a difference. And as a result, generally, we do nothing.

I hope that you will be inspired by the examples of the four friends who showed that you must first determine how much time that you can give, what talents you have, who else can be asked to join with you and how much seed money that you can provide. You see this is your "horse" and after you have determined the strength of your horse then you can determine how you can make a difference. I hope that you too will put the horse before the cart and discover, as the four friends did, that you can truly make a difference.

Don't put the cart before the horse.

__Help Only One__

A wise man was taking a sunrise walk on the beach. In the distance, he caught sight of a little girl who seemed to be dancing along the waves. As he got close, he saw the little girl picking up starfish from the sand and tossing them gently back into the ocean. "What are you doing?" the wise man asked. "The sun is coming up and the tide is going out; if I don't throw them in, they'll die." the little girl responded. "But little girl there are miles and miles of beach here with starfish all along the way, you can't possibly make a difference." The little girl bent down, picked up another starfish and threw it lovingly back into the ocean past the breaking waves. "It made a difference to that one," she replied.

The young girl's action represents something special in each and every one of us. We are all gifted with the ability to make a difference. We only need to take action.

I'm sure you've probably heard this little
story before. But its message is timeless.

Do you remember the examples that Larry
explained to the four friends about Aubyn
Burnside who simply started by collecting a
few pre-owned suitcases for foster children
in her town? Do you remember the story of
Karen Louks who started The Linus Project?
All she did at the beginning was simply knit a
few blankets for a few sick children in a hospital close to her.
Did you know that the Make a Wish
Foundation, which over the years has granted
wishes to thousands of children was started
by a mother with a sick child and a few of her
friends on the police department who granted
his wish to be a police officer before he died
of leukemia at the age of 7 years?

It's not necessary for you, however, to
think in terms of forming a large national organization. To do pro-active giving you only
have to follow the four simple steps and think
of "helping only one".

<u>One Hundred Years from Now</u>

One hundred years from now it will not matter how big my bank account was, the sort of house I lived in, or the kind of car I drove - - - but the world may be different because I was important in the life of a child.

Use Your Talents

The Parable of the Talents

In the Gospel of Matthew, Chapter 25 a parable is told about the master who gives three of his servants some talents and then leaves on a trip and when he returns asks each one of the servants what he has done to use his talents to help others. He rewards the two servants that have so used their talents but chides the third one who has done nothing. The message in the parable is clear, that each of us has been given some talents and each of us is expected to use our talents to help others.

In America today thousands of people generously give their time to volunteer to help nonprofit agencies and organizations. It amazes me however that so many thousands who do volunteer fail to match up their volunteer efforts with the talents that they have. They could do so much more, and enjoy the volunteer activity so much more if they did so.

We find retired accountants and financial executives helping to stock the shelves of a food pantry - - - we find a salesman who works one day a week in the cafeteria of the local nonprofit hospital - - - etc., etc. Volunteer activities are always a good thing and always helpful. How much more, however, would these volunteers accomplish if they matched their volunteer activities with the talents that they have and particularly with the things they enjoy doing. The financial executive could help many small nonprofits with a design of their own accounting and financial systems and to secure the most efficient computer software programs. The salesman who was very successful in sales during his lifetime could help so many small nonprofits in their approach to securing grant funds and helping them "sell their mission." If you are an avid golfer, help a local agency organize a golf tournament to raise funds.

The message is clear - - - the message is simple - - - if you want to be most effective in your charitable giving and make the largest difference in other people's lives match the talent that you have with your volunteer activities. Do the thing that you enjoy doing. You will enjoy your charitable activity so much more.

Do what you can with what you have where you are.

Theodore Roosevelt
Former President

The Power of Collaboration

Two people can always accomplish more than one person alone.

We often read about devastating forest fires that destroy thousands of acres of forest lands, often time hundreds of homes - - - and we forget that in many cases these forest fires were started by - - - one single spark.

We often feel that we can't make a difference because we fail to consider the simple powerful force of collaboration. We often forget that if we can simply be the spark to help one child, one family or one person that other people will want to join with us if we invite them to do so and together we can accomplish a lot.

As you remember the stories and examples given by Larry to the four friends, you will remember that amazing things were accomplished because one person acted as a spark to ignite others to join with him or her to make a difference in the world.

People today are anxious to help other people. Many times all they need is the invitation to join with you and the opportunity to participate in a project.

All of us have the power of collaboration as a resource. Collaboration simply mean asking a member of your family, a friend, a co-worker, or any other individual to help, asking the members of an organization or a church to join with you in a project and simply, gently leading the way for others to follow.

The greatest use of life is to spend it - - - for something that will outlast it.

Winston Churchill
Statesman

Seed Money

Have you ever seen a sunflower seed and noticed how small it was? This seed produces one of the tallest flowers.

Probably 90% of charitable giving in the United States is what is called re-active giving. We are asked, no, we are bombarded with requests to give to many different charitable causes here in America or to charities that perform services all over the world. We can't give to all of them so we usually pick one, or a few of them and make checks out, address the envelope, put the check in the envelope, put a stamp on the envelope and mail it.

Re-active charitable giving "just writing checks", will never bring you the personal satisfaction that you will get from joining your dollars with your time and talent.

Study after study has shown that unless people give to a cause that they believe in and unless they give not only some dollars, but some of their time and talent to that cause in a way that they can see the difference that they make because of their efforts, they will not realize the deep and personal satisfaction that comes from charitable giving. They will never experience the fact that it is better to give than to receive.

In re-active giving, just writing checks, the writing of the check and the amount of the check becomes the most important part of the charitable process, in fact, it is the only action taken by you.

In pro-active charitable giving and following the four simple steps, the amount of money that is provided by you is by far the least important of the four steps involved. This is because the money that is provided is simply seed money to accomplish a specific charitable mission. It is like the acorn that will allow the oak

tree to grow, it is like the sunflower seed that will grow a new sunflower and it is like the spark that may cause a bonfire to burn.

Will you be the spark that may start a bonfire?

<u>Why Not Try It?</u>

You have nothing to lose - - - but everything to gain.

Are you ready to experience for yourself the fact that "it is better to give than to receive" - - - that you will receive back more, much more than you give and that you will find a new purpose and meaning for your own life.

Why not give it a try? You really can't lose anything. But, you may gain a whole new purpose and meaning in your own life.

Man must decide for himself what will be the monument of his existence.

Viktor Frankl
Author-Holocaust Survivor

A Simple Way - - -
To Give Less Money to Charity - - -
Making a Larger Difference in the World
- - -
And Get Back More Than you Give

This book shows each of us how pro-active giving is so much more effective than just writing checks (re-active giving) and how each of us can use this to give meaning to our charitable spirit.

All of us want to feel needed and to feel important - - - that our lives make a difference - - - this book will show you how in a few simple steps.

People hunger today for a purpose and meaning to their lives - - - a purpose beyond the accumulation of more and more material goods - - - a purpose beyond mere recreation and pleasure - - - and often ask, "Why am I here, what is my purpose?" - - - the message of this book will give your life a new meaning and purpose.

About the Author

Robert O. Doucette is an attorney in Leominster, Massachusetts with a private practice focused on helping clients form non-profit organizations, helping families form family foundations, and assisting businesses to form business foundations to bring a focus and mission to their charitable giving.

Through his practice and research on effective charitable organizations, he realized that there were four simple steps that should be used by individuals, families, groups, organizations or businesses in order to be effective in their charitable giving programs.

To inspire the adoption of a pro-active giving approach, he recently formed a nonprofit corporation in Massachusetts called "A Helping Hand Foundation, Inc." and received the approval of the Internal Revenue Service to be classified as a recognized 501(c)(3) charity. The mission of this charitable foundation as described in its website: www.A-HelpingHand.org is to inspire the use of pro-active giving in order to realize the benefits that will flow to the giver and to experience the truth of the statement that, "It is better to give than to receive."

A portion of the profits from the sale of this book will be donated to the Helping Hand Foundation.